That Tree

That Tree : An iPhone Photo Journal Documenting a Year in the Life of a Lonely Bur Oak.
By Mark Hirsch

First Edition, 2013
ISBN 978-0-615-80442-2

Front cover : January 19 - Day 302. I witnessed this incredible sunset and barely got there in time to photograph it. A silhouette and a sunset may be cliché, but it was too pretty not to share!

Back cover : An awesome tree in a field I drive by on every trip to town. Shrouded in today's snowstorm, I felt compelled to hike out and make a picture of it.

Inside front flap : (Top) In pursuit of the perfect composition on a sub-zero morning, photographer Mark Hirsch lays in a frozen cornfield making a sunrise photo of That Tree.
(Bottom) Hirsch trudges through a snowy cornfield searching for that perfect vantage point. (Photos by N. Warren Winter / PSG)

Inside rear flap : (Top) Mark Hirsch pauses for a portrait with That Tree.
(Bottom) 50 feet up in That Tree, Hirsch pre-visualizes a composition in preparation for the group photo on Day 365. (Photos by N. Warren Winter / PSG)

Page 1 : That Tree prepares to weather a thunderstorm as lightning illuminates a darkening evening sky.

Page 5 : I spent an entire year photographing That Tree with my iPhone 4S. The day I made this picture, I had just activated my new iPhone 5. Even though it's not about the camera, it seems fitting that an incredible sunset would inspire me to make this photo of That Tree as my first image with my new phone.

Edited, designed and published by N. Warren Winter / PSG.

Except where otherwise credited, all photographs in this book were taken by Mark Hirsch exclusively using an iPhone 4s. Camera+ was the primary app used to capture the images and SnapSeed was used as the primary in camera app to tone the photographs.

Copies of That Tree and museum quality prints can be purchased online at www.thattree.net. To book Hirsch for speaking engagements or gallery exhibitions contact his agent at the following:

Press Syndication Group
c/o : N. Warren Winter
warren@psgwire.com
t: 646.325.3221
4141 N. Sacramento Avenue
Chicago, Illinois 60618

Printed in China.

TABLE *of* CONTENTS

Dedicated to That Tree. May your presence be forever on the horizon.

- Mark Hirsch

Foreword
By Vincent Laforet

There is an odd synergy between a tree and a photograph, made even more remarkable within the pages of this book.

While a photograph ultimately records a singular moment in time, the world captured within its four corners remains still, forever. A tree on the other hand, can often seem impervious to time, an anchor of sorts, standing tall and motionless as wind and time flows through its branches. When you combine the two, you gain a unique appreciation for both the finite and infinite nature of time.

Keep in mind that an Oak tree in particular, can live to be more than fourteen hundred years old. That tree witnesses an incredible number of seasons and life cycles while simultaneously defying them by being a quiet beacon of perseverance. A large oak tree can become shelter during life's many storms. A photograph on the other hand is more fragile, yet it is impervious to time and if properly preserved, it allows a small fraction of time to live on forever.

The value of a photograph is often linked with the historical importance of the event that was captured. Famous photographs include: Man landing on the moon, the overthrow of a regime, the shattering of an Olympic record. But as any veteran photographer will tell you, the power of some of the very best photographs is seldom obvious at first. History happens in a blink of an eye. But given time and the change associated with it, the true value of an image truly emerges. Often times, an image of the "every day" can become a fascinating study of how we as humans, and our environment have come to evolve.

As children we often take the tree in our backyard for granted, but as we grow up and return to our home, that tree can mysteriously stir up strong emotions, and memories, as we notice all of the changes that have come to surround it.

In photographing a single tree every single day for one year, Mark Hirsch has somehow managed to capture so much of this. On a simple level, the tree in and of itself, is just "that" tree. There is nothing inherently "special" about it.

Yet as we take a few moments to flip through these pages, and slow down from our increasingly distracted lives, as Mark did himself, we gain a new perspective.

We come to appreciate our mortality a bit more. We ponder whether our time on this earth, our actions, and the roots we grow can somehow last as long as that tree. That lone tree, once unnoticed now has the power to give us a little more perspective on the bigger picture of life.

It's even more remarkable that that tree can do this, by doing little, if anything, at all. That tree, just "is." Perhaps we could all learn to appreciate the beauty and power found within the simplicity of nature's plan for us all - if only by following its example, and witnessing time, as opposed to rushing through it.

In the simple act of photographing That Tree, Mark has done something remarkable: he has given That Tree true immortality.

Vincent Laforet, a three-time winner at the prestigious 2010 Cannes Lions International Advertising Festival, is a director and Pulitzer Prize–winning photographer who is known for his forward thinking approach to image making and storytelling. In addition to having been commissioned by just about every important international publication including Vanity Fair, The New York Times Magazine, National Geographic, Sports Illustrated, Time, Newsweek, and Life, Vincent is considered a pioneer both for his innovative tilt-shift and aerial photography and in the field of HD-capable DSLR cameras. You can view Vincent's work at www.laforetvisuals.com.

Introduction

Despite being a landowner, outdoors enthusiast, mountain biker, hunter and fisherman, I've never really viewed myself as an environmentalist. Those perceptions about myself changed to some degree in 2012 as the result of an unintended adventure brought about by my purchase of an iPhone.

A professional photographer by trade, my subject matter is usually editorial or marketing related. When Cori Pepelnjak, a photographer friend of mine, learned of my iPhone purchase, she suggested that I might appreciate the camera built into my new cell phone. At first I chuckled at the concept, but then I quickly embraced the simplicity of the technology, embarking on a project that has allowed me to discover a tremendous appreciation for the forest and the land.

The project, That Tree, was my commitment to make and share an iPhone photo a day for a full year on my Facebook and Instagram pages. These photos feature my visual discoveries of the finite world in and around a lonely old Bur Oak tree, all photographed using my iPhone. My adventure began when I took my first experimental images of That Tree during a January 20, 2012 snowstorm. Those first images and the feedback from two friends served as the catalyst and inspiration that motivated me to take on this challenging and rewarding project.

About two miles from my home, That Tree is situated precariously on the fringe of highly productive agricultural crop ground in a Southwest Wisconsin cornfield. My relationship with That Tree has awakened a newfound vision, and appreciation for the fragility of our world and the interdependence of even the smallest of its creatures. In turn, this fresh insight has inspired my commitment to share my photos and encourage others to embrace land stewardship as a means toward a more sustainable use of our resources.

One field trip forever etched in my memory is that of Lora Kohnlein and her two boys, Patrick, 7, and Duggan, 8. (See page 69, July 12 - Day 111) The boys and I climbed That Tree sitting there comfortably in its gnarly branches. It reminded me of my childhood days spent climbing an old maple tree with my brothers Jon, David, Andy, and my little sister Sarah in the backyard of our home in Boscobel, Wisconsin.

The long trip too, from and beneath the old oak also allowed the boys and I to discover every imaginable species of insect yielding a real-world experience that could not be duplicated in front of any TV set.

On the evening of July 2, 2012, I arrived before dusk hoping to capture That Tree silhouetted against the deep blue skies that occur just after sunset. While sitting in the waterway watching and waiting, a Barred Owl swooped in, landing in the branches of That Tree. He soon spotted me lying in the grass and made a quick departure. Then a nighthawk came strafing the grassy waterway in search of insects flying within inches of my hiding place. These are two wonderful encounters residing only as images in my minds eye.

Then as the light was getting just right, I found myself surrounded by the blinking and flashing yellow lights as a frenzy of fireflies filled the valley. I tried to make a photo using one of several camera apps I have on the iPhone, but none of them had a slow enough shutter speed to record what I was witnessing. Then with my iPhone mounted on a tripod, I tried an app called SlowShutter. When I activated the shutter, I was amazed to see a yellow paint splash of color appear capturing the fleeting trail of a firefly. Just like I would have as a young boy, I found myself running around the valley herding fireflies, giggling like a little kid. (See page 64, July 2 - Day 101)

These encounters would not have occurred if not for the preservation of That Tree and the flourishing habitat that it creates in a waterway on the fringe of a cornfield. These encounters add merit to the concept of a tree of life for I've seen first hand that this tree is the anchor, refuge, home, and oasis for countless plant and animal species. I have That Tree to thank for inspiring my project and for supporting a unique ecosystem and habitat for so many living creatures.

March 24 - Day 1 : Spindly branches, like black lightning with pastel skies and a break on the horizon.

March 25 - Day 2

March 26 - Day 3

March 27 - Day 4

March 28 - Day 5

March 29 - Day 6

March 30 - Day 7

March 31 - Day 8

Facing page : (*left to right, top to bottom*)
March 25 - Day 2 : Like desert pavement, the cracked surface of repaired waterways leads to a lonely old oak.
March 26 - Day 3 : Contrasts of color and life.
March 27 - Day 4 : Lush spring grasses contrast with the unplanted cornfield beside That Tree.
March 28 - Day 5 : That Tree shows its first signs of springing to life.

This page : (*left to right, top to bottom*)
March 29 - Day 6 : Ethereal and windy sunset.
March 30 - Day 7 : Ancient and tangled branches encircle the trunk reaching all the way to the ground.
March 31 - Day 8 : Burning bush! Getting difficult to come up with fresh perspectives. Though it appears That Tree is on fire, it's actually being illuminated by the headlights of my truck shining up the hill at its base.

April 1 - Day 9 : Like a dart, a starling flies from its perch amidst the barren branches.

April 2 - Day 10   April 3 - Day 11   April 4 - Day 12

This page : (*left to right*)
April 2 - Day 10 : Remnants from last year's homesteaders.
April 3 - Day 11 : Old wounds from time served as a fence post.
April 4 - Day 12 : Soon to be lost by a canopy filled with leaves, I decided to shoot That Tree's skeletal shadow for today's perspective.

Facing page :
April 5 - Day 13 : Slightly larger than a mouses ear, oak leaves are starting to take shape on That Tree.

April 5 - Day 13 ⟶

April 6 - Day 14

This page : (*top to bottom*)
April 6 - Day 14 : Sunlight illuminates the heart of That Tree.
April 7 - Day 15 : Flat light and short on time so today's perspective is a macro view from the south side of That Tree.

Facing page :
April 8 - Day 16 : A carpeted green waterway and fleeting cloud cover frames That Tree on the horizon.

April 7 - Day 15

April 8 - Day 16

April 9 - Day 17

April 10 - Day 18

This page : (*top to bottom*)
April 9 - Day 17 : That Tree dwarfed beneath a clear blue sky.
April 10 - Day 18 : Sunrise shadows and repeated patterns of That Tree.

Facing page :
April 11 - Day 19 : A waning moon hangs over That Tree as the first rays of sunrise paint it a blood red against the morning sky.

April 11 - Day 19

April 12 - Day 20

April 13 - Day 21

This page : (*left to right*)
April 12 - Day 20 : Silhouetted against a vibrantly colored sky, That Tree witnesses another beautiful sunrise.
April 13 - Day 21 : Like a sea creature on a bed of coral, a tiny spider hunts for prey on the mossy bark of That Tree. To appreciate the macro perspective, the spider's outstretched legs would not cover the face of a dime.

Facing page :
April 14 - Day 22 : I never know what visual discovery I might make in my ever expanding field of view around That Tree. Kind of like life!

April 14 - Day 22

April 15 - Day 23

April 16 - Day 24

This page : (*top to bottom*)
April 15 - Day 23 : Details, details.
April 16 - Day 24 : Standing atop an oasis of green on a gloomy Monday morning, That Tree overlooks the still brown and unplanted cornfields.

Facing page :
April 17 - Day 25 : That Tree's shadow is cast on a barren agricultural landscape once dominated by tall grass prairie.

April 17 - Day 25

April 18 - Day 26

April 19 - Day 27

This page : (*left to right, top to bottom*)
April 18 - Day 26 : Sculpted by a corn planter, furrows lead to a sentinel of the prairie.
April 19 - Day 27 : A strong presence in sunlight or shadow, That Tree dominates the horizon.
April 20 - Day 28 : Spring rains inspired a drive to That Tree and a fresh perspective from the comfort of my pickup truck.

Facing page :
April 21 - Day 29 : Discovered remnants and the heart of a future oak.

April 20 - Day 28

April 21 - Day 29

April 22 - Day 30

April 23 - Day 31

This page : (*left to right*)
April 22 - Day 30 : New leaves unfurl on a long lived branch encrusted in lichen and mosses.
April 23 - Day 31 : A fallen leaf wrapped in the flow of wind blown grasses.

Facing page :
April 24 - Day 32 : A cool discovery, spring's rebirth and a clutch of wild turkey eggs.

April 24 - Day 32

This page : (*clockwise from top right*)

April 25 - Day 33 : That Tree with a crescent moon and the planet Venus just after sunset.

April 26 - Day 34 : A tiny blade of grass grows from a crack in the gnarly bark of That Tree.

April 27 - Day 35 : Break of day.

April 28 - Day 36 : Textured bark, green grass, and a remnant from days serving as a fence post.

April 29 - Day 37 : A canopy of new leaves glows golden with dawn's early light.

April 25 - Day 33

April 29 - Day 37

April 28 - Day 36

April 27 - Day 35

April 26 - Day 34

April 30 - Day 38

Previous page :
April 30 - Day 38 : A foggy morning flyover.

Facing page:
May 1 - Day 39 : Vibrant green leaves of That Tree are cast against a bright foggy background.

May 2 - Day 40

May 3 - Day 41

May 4 - Day 42

May 5 - Day 43

This page : (*left to right, top to bottom*)
May 2 - Day 40 : Where fences fall, That Tree endures.
May 3 - Day 41 : The moon rise framed by gnarly dead branches of That Tree.
May 4 - Day 42 : The amber glow of sunset shines through casting mottled shadows on That Tree.
May 5 - Day 43 : Pastel crayon sunset.

Facing page :
May 6 - Day 44 : Translucent colors, natural patterns, and shapes revealed.

May 6 - Day 44

This page : (*top to bottom, left to right*)

May 7 - Day 45 : From a bumblebee's perspective amidst the dandelions.

May 8 - Day 46 : Witnessing another dawn with my back against That Tree.

May 9 - Day 47 : A blazing sky at sunset.

May 10 - Day 48 : A sparrow pauses amidst the protective branches of That Tree.

Facing page :

May 11 - Day 49 : Like a desert landscape painted red by sunset. Shadows revisited with old dead branches reaching out like bony fingers.

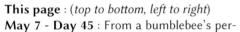

May 7 - Day 45

May 8 - Day 46

May 9 - Day 47

May 10 - Day 48

May 11 - Day 49

May 12 - Day 50

(*left to right, top to bottom*)
May 12 - Day 50 : Me and That Tree.
May 13 - Day 51 : Tiny corn seedlings sur-rounding That Tree are highlighted by the setting sun.
May 14 - Day 52 : Reaching up and down.

May 13 - Day 51

May 14 - Day 52

May 15 - Day 53

May 15 - Day 53 : A golden sunrise shines through the leaves of That Tree.
May 16 - Day 54 : Holding up a full canopy of leaves, That Tree basks in the warm glow of sunrise.
May 17 - Day 55 : That Tree witnesses the dawn of another day.

May 16 - Day 54

May 17 - Day 55

May 18 - Day 56 : Bathed in the warm glow of first light.

May 19 - Day 57

May 20 - Day 58

May 21 - Day 59

Previous pages : (*left to right*)
May 19 - Day 57 : Veined leaves coursing with the energy of captured sunlight.
May 20 - Day 58 : A lone wildflower emerges from the tall grasses surrounding That Tree.

This page : (*left to right, top to bottom*)
May 21 - Day 59 : Stalking That Tree through tall grass.
May 22 - Day 60 : Embraced by the heart of her branches.
May 23 - Day 61 : Reminiscent of prairies past.
May 24 - Day 62 : Gnarly branches illuminated by golden light.

Facing page :
May 25 - Day 63 : That Tree stands atop a wind whipped sea of undulating green grasses during last night's wind storm.

May 22 - Day 60

May 23 - Day 61

May 24 - Day 62

May 25 - Day 63

May 26 - Day 64 : Guess this is why at least one of the many birds is always squawking at me by That Tree.

May 27 - Day 65

May 28 - Day 66

May 29 - Day 67

This page : (*top to bottom, left to right*)
May 27 - Day 65 : After the rain, lush and green!
May 28 - Day 66 : Tiny acorns and the hearts of future oaks are forming.
May 29 - Day 67 : The start of a good morning.
May 30 - Day 68 : Already a foot tall, converging rows of corn plants will soon obscure the view of That Tree.

Facing page :
May 31 - Day 69 : An experimental mix of dusk light and off camera flash helped capture this grainy and painterly scene.

May 30 - Day 68

May 31 - Day 69

This page : (*left to right, top to bottom*)
June 1 - Day 70 : Invasive sweet clover dominates the waterway below That Tree.
June 2 - Day 71 : Me, That Tree, and the light from a gorgeous red sunset.
June 3 - Day 72 : Beneath wispy clouds and blue skies, drought stressed vegetation exhibits a yellow shade of green.
June 4 - Day 73 : The day departs with a watercolor sunset.

Facing page :
June 5 - Day 74 : A semi-healthy oak leaf is framed by the lacy holes left in another leaf by insects or herbicide damage on That Tree.

June 2 - Day 71

June 1 - Day 70

June 3 - Day 72

June 4 - Day 73

June 5 - Day 74

June 6 - Day 75 : A dawn scene of That Tree with the full moon looming above.

June 7 - Day 76

June 8 - Day 77

This page: (*left to right, top to bottom*)
June 7 - Day 76 : A herbicide applicator adds to That Tree's precarious existence.
June 8 - Day 77 : Shared a gorgeous sunrise and the dawn of another day in the company of That Tree.
June 9 - Day 78 : Sunsets, shadows and silhouettes.

Facing page:
June 10 - Day 79 : A rainbow of light at sunrise.

June 9 - Day 78

June 10 - Day 79

June 11 - Day 80   June 12 - Day 81

This page : (*left to right*)
June 11 - Day 80 : The lavender sky from last night's sunset is framed by leaves of That Tree which are damaged from either insects or disease.
June 12 - Day 81 : That Tree is framed by blue skies and tall corn on another beautiful morning.

Facing page :
June 13 - Day 82 : A John Deere tractor and That Tree are silhouetted against the cool blue sky of dusk as Craig Rees cuts the hay crop in the waterway between the cornfields.

June 13 - Day 82 ⟶

June 14 - Day 83

This page : (*left to right, top to bottom*)
June 14 - Day 83 : Leaf shadows and tree textures.
June 15 - Day 84 : Fresh baled hay on a humid summer day.
June 16 - Day 85 : A familiar profile hidden behind a curtain of grasses.
June 17 - Day 86 : Sunlight breaks through the clouds illuminating That Tree against a foggy backdrop at sunrise. Happy Father's Day!

June 15 - Day 84

June 16 - Day 85

June 17 - Day 86

June 18 - Day 87

June 19 - Day 88

June 20 - Day 89

June 21 - Day 90

This page : (*left to right, top to bottom*)
June 18 - Day 87 : The setting sun casts a golden glow on the landscape surrounding That Tree.

June 19 - Day 88 : Another day's outcome from my visual wrestling match with That Tree.

June 20 - Day 89 : Shining in the morning light, That Tree stands boldly over a thriving corn crop.

June 21 - Day 90 : That Tree glows against a backlit scene of blue sky and cumulus clouds.

Next pages : (*left to right*)
June 22 - Day 91 : Shadows, textures, and silhouette.

June 23 - Day 92 : A backlit leaf is highlighted by a sunburst.

June 22 - Day 91

June 23 - Day 92

June 24 - Day 93

June 28 - Day 97

June 25 - Day 94

This page : (*clockwise from top left*)
June 24 - Day 93 : Body armor.
June 25 - Day 94 : Corn plants spiked from lack of moisture frame That Tree against a horizon lit by the warm glow of sunset.
June 26 - Day 95 : Dusk, That Tree, and a crescent moon.
June 27 - Day 96 : I started my day with That Tree and a gorgeous sunrise. You should have been there too!
June 28 - Day 97 : The silhouetted leaves of That Tree frame a brilliant blue and cloud filled sky at sunrise.

June 27 - Day 96

June 26 - Day 95

June 29 - Day 98

Previous page :
June 29 - Day 98 : Discovering something as simple as a clover blossom in the shadow of That Tree gives me pause to appreciate the beauty of simple things.

This page :
June 30 - Day 99 : Ominous clouds loomed over That Tree when a storm blew through yesterday afternoon just before I left for a photo shoot in Milwaukee. Too bad it didn't share a drop or two of rain.

July 1 - Day 100

July 2 - Day 101

(left to right, top to bottom)

July 1 - Day 100 : With That Tree standing in the background, a robin perches on the branch of an old dead elm just down the valley.

July 2 - Day 101 : What a cool experience tonight! Reminds me of when I was a kid chasing fireflies. I had my iPhone on a tripod and I was running around the field trying to catch fireflies when an owl swoops in and lands in That Tree. I made a stealthy retreat back to my iPhone but the owl flew away before I could shoot a photo. Another nice image residing only in my mind eye.

July 3 - Day 102 : That Tree is framed by gracefully arched corn leaves.

July 3 - Day 102

July 4 - Day 103

July 5 - Day 104

July 6 - Day 105

(*left to right, top to bottom*)

July 4 - Day 103 : It was a challenge to create a July 4 image since fireworks would be a bad idea due to the dry conditions. My alternative, treat a flag like a filter, overexpose, and shoot the backlit tree as a silhouette.

July 5 - Day 104 : That Tree resides on it's own little island in the corn.

July 6 - Day 105 : The setting sun shines it's last light of day.

July 7 - Day 106

July 8 - Day 107

July 9 - Day 108

This page : (*top to bottom, left to right*)

July 7 - Day 106 : That Tree witnesses the cool blue skies of dawn which will soon yield to sweltering heat and drought like conditions.

July 8 - Day 107 : The view from high within the strength of That Tree's sweeping branches.

July 9 - Day 108 : A beautiful day departed with a comforting sunset.

July 10 - Day 109 : Awash in the warm glow of evening light, That Tree is cast against the watercolor sky of dusk.

Next page :

July 11 - Day 110 : The fading light of day breaks through thick foliage to paint itself in mottled patches on the trunk and branches of That Tree.

July 10 - Day 109

July 11 - Day 110

July 12 - Day 111 : Visiting from Henderson, Colorado, I had a fun time early this morning introducing Lora Kohnlein and her sons Duggan, 8, (left) and Patrick, 7, (right) to That Tree. The boys and I climbed the tree, examined dozens of bugs and discussed the finer points of the video game Angry Birds. Thanks boys for inspiring me to see things like a kid again!

July 13 - Day 112

This page : (*left to right, top to bottom*)
July 13 - Day 112 : Cumulus clouds capture and hold the brilliant light of sunset.
July 14 - Day 113 : The drought persists with cloud free skies.
July 15 - Day 114 : Managed to stop by That Tree for a foggy perspective at 5:30 a.m..
July 16 - Day 115 : Sunrise!

Facing Page :
July 17 - Day 116 : Clinging to it's bark, an interesting resident of That Tree and it's surrounding habitat glows in a shaft of sunlight.

July 14 - Day 113

July 15 - Day 114

July 16 - Day 115

July 17 - Day 116

July 18 - Day 117

July 19 - Day 118

July 20 - Day 119

This page : (*top to bottom, left to right*)

July 18 - Day 117 : A painted sunset is framed by the drought withered leaves of That Tree and corn plants spiked from lack of moisture.

July 19 - Day 118 : And the rains finally came.

July 20 - Day 119 : Another inhabitant blending into That Tree's world.

July 21 - Day 120 : The warm glow of sunrise reflects a subtle glow onto a still life of cast off remnants at the base of That Tree.

July 22 - Day 121 : With That Tree silhouetted on the horizon, the setting sun illuminates blossoms of Queen Anne's Lace.

July 21 - Day 120

July 22 - Day 121

July 23 - Day 122

The Blackbirds
Shadowy Sentinels of That Tree

For a full year, I made my daily forays through the cornfields to photograph an ancient lonely bur oak tree. It was a very solitary, quiet, and contemplative experience of oneness within the realm of That Tree.

Other than insects and an occasional songbird, I saw very little visible wildlife. The one creature I had the most interaction with though were the blackbirds, the shadowy sentinels of That Tree's realm. Their presence served as an occasional reminder that I was not necessarily a welcomed visitor.

Early on in the project, they would flit from plant to plant following me with a chorus of unapproving squawks as I made my hike through the fields to That Tree. Like a relay team, new blackbirds would take over along the way with the task of chattering a reminder of their disapproval as I made my way through the cornfield. Even when I arrived at the tree, they would continue to squawk and swoop at me in an effort to discourage my presence. The displeased and impatient blackbirds never stayed still long enough to allow me to capture their form in a composition or portrait.

> *"The one creature I had the most interaction*
> *with though were the blackbirds,*
> *the shadowy sentinels of That Tree's realm."*

One of my favorite pictures from the project features a single blackbird I photographed darting from the stark barren branches against a neutral overcast sky. (April 1, Page 13) Another features a single blackbird on a particularly foggy morning breaking from the mist as it did a flyover surveying my departure from of the valley of That Tree. (See page 29, April 30 - Day 38)

As the days went by, my trips to That Tree became quieter. I heard the owls in the distance or the songbirds in the neighboring forests. At dusk and dawn, I experienced the distant yips and howls of the coyotes or the rare song of a thrush or whippoorwill down the valley. Though I would still see them observing me from their swaying perch in the grasses, the cacophony and chatter of the blackbirds had finally disappeared.

Two days from the conclusion of my project, I was up well before dawn setting up my tripod to frame a composition of That Tree between some remnant corn plants that had evaded the fall harvest. I mounted my camera and sat down in the snow and ice to wait for the arrival of the sunrise.

In a scene I have witnessed many times over the past year, the sun began to paint it's crimson light from tip to trunk over That Tree. And just as the sunlight washed it's warm glow over the corn plants in the foreground of my composition, a nearby blackbird began singing it's harmonious welcome to the sunrise and to me.

The Deer
Take Only Pictures, Leave Only Footprints

During my yearlong project to document the life of That Tree, I made many pictures and yes, I left many footprints. I also carry many memories of experiences that were never translated into photographs.

As I spent the year making my various and repeated treks to photograph That Tree, I developed a pattern and approach as I sought to reduce the presence of my footprints on the landscape. This became even more difficult during the long winter season since I did not want my footprints in the snow to be part of my visual record.

After one of the few rain showers that occurred during my project and the drought of 2012, I discovered that my quiet path through the cornfield was being mirrored by the white-tailed deer. Based on their footprints over mine, it seemed my path of least resistance and my direction of approach was the same path the deer followed to reach That Tree. Though I never saw them, their hoof prints were always there leading me through the cornfield.

With a heavy fog hanging in the valley, I arrived before sunrise one morning hoping to capture a photograph of the deer grazing on acorns and fresh grasses beneath That Tree. I made a stealthy approach and found a spot to hide on the fringe of the cornfield. Soon I spotted their tiny figures as a pair of yearlings chased one another through the grassy waterway down the valley from where I hid. Like shadowy ghosts, they darted in and out of the mist, playful figures dancing on ethereal clouds disappearing as quickly as they appeared.

I arrived early on another crisp fall morning making a pre-dawn discovery of a frosty leaf resting in the spiked fingers of a frosty patch of grass. I lay down in the grass beside the natural still life, mounted my iPhone on my tripod, and waited for the sunrise to break over the horizon.

The sun soon appeared highlighting my frosty composition. (October 27, Day 218) I was constantly shifting, but only slightly, trying to capture just the right quality of light. The higher the sun rose, the lower I shifted my perspective. I worked it for quite some time until I thought I finally had the image I was looking for.

I lay there for so long that my back became stiff and my knees were killing me. Eventually, I stood up to stretch. When I turned towards the tree, I witnessed what would have been another fantastic photo opportunity.

That Tree was 30 yards away from me, and between us stood a beautiful and startled 10-point white-tailed buck. Unfortunately, in this case, it was I who was the proverbial deer caught in the headlights. With my iPhone still mounted in the grips of my tripod, I could only watch as he made a hasty retreat.

Though I frequently encountered other signs of their shared presence in the realm of That Tree, photographically the deer remained elusive. Despite never capturing their photographs, it was very comforting to know that the deer found the valley to be a safe and healthy place to exist.

This project inspired me to see things with a greater appreciation and a more considered eye. It also gave me memorable moments of incredible fascination like those of the white-tailed deer that didn't always translate into photographs. Though they are only memories, I carry them with me, and there they will remain long after the rains have washed away our shared footprints on the quiet pathway to That Tree.

July 24 - Day 123

July 25 - Day 124

July 26 - Day 125

Page 73 :
July 23 - Day 122 : A cloud break on the horizon delivered a brief but dramatic sunset.

This page : (*left to right, top to bottom*)
July 24 - Day 123 : Crossroads on my back in a nettles patch.
July 25 - Day 124 : A gorgeous and cool morning to witness the sunrise.
July 26 - Day 125 : Out 'til wee hours of the morn trying to capture lightning with That Tree. Lots of washed out skies and one tiny bolt.
July 27 - Day 126 : The sweeping light of sunset casts a contrasty glow over That Tree and a drought stressed corn crop.

Facing page :
July 28 - Day 127 : Discovered this guy at That Tree hanging out at 5:30 a.m. in the warm rays of sunrise.

July 27 - Day 126

July 28 - Day 127

July 31 - Day 130

(*clockwise from top right*)

July 29 - Day 128 : Maybe the cold blue dawn will yield some much needed rain, or not.

July 30 - Day 129 : A break in the clouds silhouettes That Tree against another nice sunset.

July 31 - Day 130 : The mottled light of sunset casts the shadow of a corn stalk onto the trunk of That Tree.

July 29 - Day 128

July 30 - Day 129

August 3 - Day 133

August 1 - Day 131

(clockwise from top right)
August 1 - Day 131 : That Tree is dwarfed by a vast blue sky.
August 2 - Day 132 : The setting sun shines it's golden contrasty light onto That Tree.
August 3 - Day 133 : Another generation!

August 2 - Day 132

August 4 - Day 134 : Full moon at sunrise.

August 4 - Day 134

August 5 - Day 135

August 6 - Day 136

This page : (*left to right*)
August 5 - Day 135 : A fallen leaf rests amidst acorns on the drought parched grass beneath That Tree.
August 6 - Day 136 : First light.

Facing page :
August 7 - Day 137 : Enjoyed a sunset with two of my favorite subjects, Magnum and That Tree.

August 7 - Day 137 ⟶

August 8 - Day 138

August 9 - Day 139

August 10 - Day 140

August 12 - Day 142

(*clockwise from top left*)

August 8 - Day 138 : Silhouetted by a stark composition at sunset.

August 9 - Day 139 : Deadly nightshade (Solanum dulcamara), also called bitter-sweet, scarletberry, and a large number of other names.

August 10 - Day 140 : Just an ordinary morning.

August 11 - Day 141 : Acorn hulls and morning light found near the base of That Tree.

August 12 - Day 142 : A storm front blows in looming over That Tree hopefully carrying some much needed precipitation. Let it rain!

August 11 - Day 141

August 13 - Day 143

August 14 - Day 144

August 15 - Day 145

August 17 - Day 147

August 16 - Day 146

(*clockwise from top left*)

August 13 - Day 143 : Drought damaged and dying corn surrounds That Tree. I was out there at 5:30 a.m. hoping to photograph a beautiful sunrise that never came and discovered this sad but colorful scene.

August 14 - Day 144 : Gold nuggets waiting to be discovered by the deer, turkeys, and squirrels.

August 15 - Day 145 : Dawns very early light.

August 16 - Day 146 : A fallen leaf from That Tree is caught in the flow of wind blown grass following a needed rainstorm.

August 17 - Day 147 : A sweet sunrise!

August 18 - Day 148

August 19 - Day 149

August 20 - Day 150

August 21 - Day 151

Previous pages : *(left to right)*
August 18 - Day 148 : The scourge of anything green, a Japanese beetle feeds on the leaves of That Tree.
August 19 - Day 149 : Drought scorched corn, That Tree, and golden light.

This page : *(clockwise from top left)*
August 20 - Day 150 : An acorn lies beneath the cover of a canopy of grass at the base of That Tree.
August 21 - Day 151 : Morning glow!
August 22 - Day 152 : Dead weeds frame That Tree in a distorted composition of scale.

Facing Page :
August 23 - Day 153 : Lens flare exaggerates the sunburst.

August 22 - Day 152

August 23 - Day 153

(*top to bottom, left to right*)

August 24 - Day 154 : Warm light and blue skies at sunset.

August 25 - Day 155 : A rainbow of color.

August 26 - Day 156 : A rain drop hangs from a branch of That Tree following a much needed rain shower.

August 27 - Day 157 : Shrouded in fog.

August 28 - Day 158 : In a drought where nothing survives, the goldenrod thrives.

August 24 - Day 154

August 25 - Day 155

August 26 - Day 156

August 27 - Day 157

August 28 - Day 158

August 29 - Day 159

August 30 - Day 160

August 31 - Day 161

(*counter clockwise from top left*)

August 29 - Day 159 : A grand tree silhouetted against a colorful sunset.

August 30 - Day 160 : It was a gorgeous morning to welcome the golden light of sunrise.

August 31 - Day 161 : A late season corn volunteer grows next to the gnarly trunk of That Tree.

September 1 - Day 162 : It has been an ugly overcast day so I decided to shoot with Hipstamatic using John S Lens, and Ina's 1969 Film.

September 1 - Day 162

September 2 - Day 163

September 5 - Day 166

September 3 - Day 164

This page : (*clockwise from upper left*)
September 2 - Day 163 : The weathered texture and sweeping branches of That Tree are lit by the warm glow of sunrise.
September 3 - Day 164 : Corn shadows at sunrise.
September 4 - Day 165 : Emerging from misty dawn.
September 5 - Day 166 : After a stormy night, the mid-morning light casts mottled shadows onto That Tree.

Facing page :
September 6 - Day 167 : "Walk me out in the morning dew my honey, walk me out in the morning dew today." -The Grateful Dead

September 4 - Day 165

September 6 - Day 167 ⟶

September 7 - Day 168

September 8 - Day 169

September 9 - Day 170

September 10 - Day 171

September 11 - Day 172

September 12 - Day 173

This page : (*left to right, top to bottom*)
September 7 - Day 168 : Managed to capture the only sunshine and a patch of blue sky after my 9 a.m. photo shoot.
September 8 - Day 169 : Hello sunrise!
September 9 - Day 170 : I finally found time for a gorgeous sunset visit to That Tree.
September 10 - Day 171 : Drought stressed leaves backlit by the sunrise.
September 11 - Day 172 : While searching for today's photo, I discovered these tiny daisy fleabane blossoms. Half the diameter of a dime, they were so small that I've walked over them unnoticed on many of my previous visits. Fortunately they caught my attention today.
September 12 - Day 173 : Chaotic and busy day. Had to settle for a sunset.

Facing page :
September 13 - Day 174 : Hanging around like an ornament on That Tree.

September 13 - Day 174

September 14 - Day 175

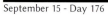
September 15 - Day 176

September 17 - Day 178

September 16 - Day 177

(*clockwise from top left*)
September 14 - Day 175 : Fog settles around That Tree at dawn.
September 15 - Day 176 : Blue skies, green grass and a burst of sunlight.
September 16 - Day 177 : Dawn silhouettes.
September 17 - Day 178 : In an early morning view before the sun succumbed to the clouds, That Tree stands out on a sea of gold.

September 18 - Day 179

September 19 - Day 180

September 21 - Day 182

September 20 - Day 181

(*clockwise from top left*)

September 18 - Day 179 : A revisited composition dwarfs That Tree beneath a cumulus filled sky.

September 19 - Day 180 : I didn't intend to shoot the sunrise but Dence mentioned the light was nice so I dashed out and managed to shoot just one frame before it was gone.

September 20 - Day 181 : That Tree is silhouetted against last night's dusky blue sky as a storm front moved through.

September 21 - Day 182 : Extraterrestrial lighting.

September 22 - Day 183

September 23 - Day 184

Previous pages : (*left to right*)
September 22 - Day 183 : Today is the halfway point for my project and the last shot with corn standing in the field. The corn gets picked this afternoon.
September 23 - Day 184 : A hard frost adorns the fringes of a leaf on That Tree. A sign of season's change with winter on the horizon.

This page : (*clockwise from middle left*)
September 24 - Day 185 : Misty sunlight is diffracted through the leaves.
September 25 - Day 186 : Starkly contrasted by clouds and sky.
September 26 - Day 187 : The warm light of sunset enhances the golden color of the corn crop waiting to be harvested near That Tree.
September 27 - Day 188 : I shot a similar composition on July 5 - Day 104. Quite a contrast!

September 25 - Day 186

September 24 - Day 185

September 27 - Day 188

September 26 - Day 187

September 28 - Day 189

September 29 - Day 190

September 30 - Day 191

Previous page :
September 28 - Day 189 : Fall delivers brilliant complimentary colors.

This page : (*left to right, top to bottom*)
September 29 - Day 190 : Victims of a hard frost, shriveled milkweed plants frame That Tree on the horizon.
September 30 - Day 191 : Sunrise breaks over the ridge line.
October 1 - Day 192 : A gorgeous sunrise is framed by the branches of That Tree. The sun has already given way to a gloomy overcast sky. I'm glad I was up to witness first light in the company of That Tree.

Facing page :
October 2 - Day 193 : Golden leaves frame That Tree in the distance.

October 1 - Day 192

October 2 - Day 193

October 3 - Day 194

October 4 - Day 195

October 5 - Day 196

October 6 - Day 197

This page : (*left to right, top to bottom*)
October 3 - Day 194 : Hard silhouettes and contrasting colors.
October 4 - Day 195 : A colorful leaf is backlit by the sunset.
October 5 - Day 196 : Illuminated by the setting sun, That Tree emits a warm glow against the evening sky.
October 6 - Day 197 : Dawn's early light.
October 7 - Day 198 : Cornfield perspectives.
October 8 - Day 199 : Happy Birthday to me!

Facing page :
October 9 - Day 200 : Probably one of my last shots with corn still standing in the field. It should be picked today or tomorrow so I wanted to shoot one last sunset with the field of gold.

October 7 - Day 198

October 8 - Day 199

October 9 - Day 200

October 10 - Day 201

October 11 - Day 202

October 12 - Day 203

October 13 - Day 204

October 14 - Day 205

October 15 - Day 206

(*left to right, top to bottom*)

October 10 - Day 201 : I shot this photo at sunrise and then met my friend and pilot Adam Pick at the airport. Unfortunately, a huge cloud bank blew in and the light was gone. Worse yet, I got motion sickness. Sucks! So here is my alternative image.

October 11 - Day 202 : It was another gorgeous morning to enjoy watching the sunrise in the company of That Tree.

October 12 - Day 203 : Emanating a cranberry red glow, the backlit leaves of That Tree frame a beautiful fall sunrise.

October 13 - Day 204 : Spent about four hours chasing the combine around the cornfield east of That Tree when all the pieces came together just before sunset.

October 14 - Day 205 : In a scene painted with the colorful contrast of fall's decay, That Tree is silhouetted against a misty horizon.

October 15 - Day 206 : First light paints the leaves of That Tree crimson red against a cold blue sky.

October 16 - Day 207

October 17 - Day 208

October 18 - Day 209

(*left to right, top to bottom*)
October 16 - Day 207 : Dawn light, fall colors and the natural pattern of things.
October 17 - Day 208 : Just another lovely sunset!
October 18 - Day 209 : That Tree, veiled in a morning gloom, with harvest remnants like battlefield carnage.

October 19 - Day 210 : Spinning, floating and rising, a leaf dances like a butterfly on the wind.

October 20 - Day 211

This page : (*top to bottom*)
October 20 - Day 211 : A quick foggy sunrise photo shoot on my way out of town for the Beechwood Blaster mountain bike race.
October 21 - Day 212 : Their days numbered by the season, sunrise backlights a thin canopy of tenacious leaves.

Facing page :
October 22 - Day 213 : The scene probably reflects the mood of the day. A bit gloomy. Happy Monday.

October 21 - Day 212

October 22 - Day 213

October 23 - Day 214

October 24 - Day 215

October 25 - Day 216

This page : (*top to bottom, left to right*)
October 23 - Day 214 : The stark aftermath following yesterday's storm, barely a leaf left on the branches of That Tree.
October 24 - Day 215 : Dawn breaks stark and somber.
October 25 - Day 216 : Sinewy bending branches frame a colorful end of day.
October 26 - Day 217 : First light paints it's amber hues on winding rows in the harvested cornfield.

Facing page :
October 27 - Day 218 : Backlit by the warm glow of sunrise, a leaf from That Tree rests in a frosty embrace.

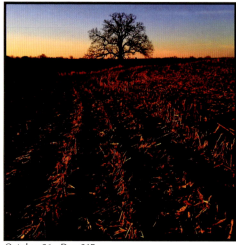

October 26 - Day 217

October 27 - Day 218

This page : (*left to right*)
October 28 - Day 219 : That Tree stands amidst a landscape shrouded in a frosty pall.
October 29 - Day 220 : The lavender skies of dusk greet the moonrise over That Tree.

Facing page :
October 30 - Day 221 : Boney!

October 28 - Day 219

October 29 - Day 220

October 30 - Day 221 ⟶

October 31 - Day 222

November 1 - Day 223

November 2 - Day 224

November 3 - Day 225

November 4 - Day 226

Previous page : (*left to right*)
October 31 - Day 222 : Moonlight shines through the gnarly branches of That Tree. Happy Halloween! This shot really pushed the technical limitations of the iPhone as you can tell.
November 1 - Day 223 : Foxtail, That Tree, and the fading light of sunset.

This page : (*clockwise from top left*)
November 2 - Day 224 : With a waning moon hanging in the sky, the sunrise paints its way across the horizon.
November 3 - Day 225 : Dawn's early light broke pleasantly pale and pastel over That Tree.
November 4 - Day 226 : A sliver of warm color that quickly faded to another gray day.
November 5 - Day 227 : I was gone before sunrise for an assignment photographing President Obama and Bruce Springsteen in Madison, Wisconsin. I barely had time to visit That Tree. The best I could do was catch a sunset. Fortunately for me it was a rather attractive one.

November 5 - Day 227

November 6 - Day 228 ⟶

November 7 - Day 229

November 8 - Day 230

November 9 - Day 231

Previous page :
November 6 - Day 228 : That Tree is reflected and inverted in the heavy wet snowflakes melted onto my truck window.

This page : (*left to right*)
November 7 - Day 229 : Remnants II.
November 8 - Day 230 : That Tree is framed by a window in the clouds.
November 9 - Day 231 : Against a blue sky at dusk, the gnarly branches of That Tree are highlighted in the red glow of sunset.

November 10 - Day 232

November 11 - Day 233

November 12 - Day 234

November 13 - Day 235

(left to right, top to bottom)

November 10 - Day 232 : Lichen radiate the warm light of sunrise against an indigo sky.

November 11 - Day 233 : That Tree stands over a sea of undulating grasses on a blustery overcast fall morning.

November 12 - Day 234 : I made this morning's photo while being interviewed and video taped for a story by Tim Elliot with NBC 15 out of Madison, Wisconsin.

November 13 - Day 235 : Bold frost crystals encrust blades of grass cradling a fallen leaf from That Tree.

November 14 - Day 236

This page : (*left to right, top to bottom*)
November 14 - Day 236 : That Tree on a flat gray day.

November 15 - Day 237 : Silhouetted against a golden sunrise, immature acorns still cling to the otherwise barren branches of That Tree.

November 16 - Day 238 : I missed the best light of the morning sitting in front of the TV watching Tim Elliott's story about my project but I still managed to get out in time to catch the last glimmer of the sunrise's golden light.

November 17 - Day 239 : Golden light to start the day.

Facing page :
November 18 - Day 240 : A leaf from That Tree is woven into the palette of nature's frosty canvas. A discovery that made me smile in awe at the wondrous happenings of nature's creations.

November 15 - Day 237

November 16 - Day 238

November 17 - Day 239

November 18 - Day 240

November 19 - Day 241

(*left to right, top to bottom*)
November 19 - Day 241 : A little sunlight and color briefly break through today's gloomy sky.
November 20 - Day 242 : A sentinel in the mist, watching over prairies vanished.
November 21 - Day 243 : Dew drops deposited by the heavy fog hang from the extraterrestrial fingers of That Tree.

November 20 - Day 242

November 21 - Day 243

November 25 - Day 247

(*counter clockwise from bottom left*)
November 22 - Day 244 : Happy Thanks-giving!

November 23 - Day 245 : Last night's crazy cool sunset! Much prettier than this morning's cold gray sky.

November 24 - Day 246 : The soft warm glow of first light.

November 25 - Day 247 : A brilliant sunrise framed by a strong framework.

November 22 - Day 244

November 23 - Day 245

November 24 - Day 246

Inspiration
Lessons Learned From That Tree

Finding inspiration can sometimes be a challenge. For me, inspiration comes from many places. My personal drive, a friend's challenge, or just about anywhere really. For my project about That Tree, a trio of friends, an unassuming old oak tree, and the simplicity of the iPhone camera inspired me.

The year 2006 ended with a major personal challenge when I lost my job of 19 years. I had been employed as a photojournalist at a respectable regional newspaper for the better part of my career working my way through the ranks to a management position. Losing my job was the most difficult experience I ever had.

Getting nudged out of your comfort zone can drag you down or inspire you to rise to the occasion. I spent the next two years covering news assignments for picture agencies like Getty Images, The Associated Press, Bloomberg News, and WireImage. I also began building a commercial photography business. My goal was to work smarter, not harder.

The challenge of losing my job made me embrace a more open-minded perspective about my photography. I had always viewed myself as "just a photographer", which is a rather silly view of one's self. It took the unintended adventure of photographing an old oak tree every day for a year to help me realize some things about myself. That Tree and the reaction of a worldwide community of very dedicated followers taught me an important lesson. First, it taught me how fortunate I am to be able to see the world the way I do. Next, it taught me that I am not just a photographer. That Tree taught me that I am a storyteller and an artist.

I truly believe that everyone has hidden talents waiting to be discovered. Some of us never display those talents to the world for fear of rejection. Others have yet to discover their hidden talents. My friend Warren Winter once said, "While curiosity may have killed the cat, it was self doubt that killed the artist." Don't let the fear of rejection, self doubt or the comfort zones of life prevent you from challenging yourself to discover your own latent talent.

"Don't act your age" is another important lesson That Tree has taught me. Over the last year I found myself doing things that others might consider absurd for a 52 year old man. My friends would say I've never really acted my age, but That Tree helped me appreciate this behavior as a good thing. Over the course of this project, I spent many sunrises and sunsets lying in the wet dewy grass, rolling around looking for the perfect camera angle in a muddy cornfield, or lying for an hour in a foot of fresh snow waiting for the sunrise. Passers by may have thought I'd had a heart attack.

I've climbed to the top of That Tree too many times to count, and I've run around the valley of That Tree flapping my arms like a madman herding fireflies. And the best part is, I didn't care how silly or foolish I looked. I was comfortable with myself, and my actions always rewarded me with something, be it a photograph or a simple, temporary escape from reality.

Through one of the driest summers on record and a winter season that lasted from October through March, I was out there in the best and worst of it. Every day, sometimes on multiple visits, I could be found chasing the light or the weather in search of my daily photograph. The weather proved to be incredibly inspiring. Like a mountain climber conquering Everest, 2012's most brutal weather conditions taught me to love mother nature's unpredictability. Just like the challenge of exploring your creative potential, I would encourage you to put on your slicker, and bundle up in your goose down jacket. When the weather is at its worst, go exploring in a world that will nudge you out of your comfort zone.

I hope others might learn from my experience and choose to get out of their comfort zone. If you've always wanted to try painting, go for it. If you like to draw, just draw. Art is a very personal thing. If you like what you create, that is all that matters.

History
That Tree Through The Generations

Lucius Lyons, a surveyor with the Public Land Survey, gazed upon the rolling hills of Grant County, in Southwest Wisconsin. The year was 1832 and the land he saw consisted of a rolling terrain carpeted in tall prairie grasses interspersed with sporadic stands of oak trees. Though the topography remains the same, the land today looks very different. The oak savannas are gone. A patchwork quilt of contoured stands of corn and soybeans have replaced the prairie grasses.

Lyons was tasked with mapping out southwestern Wisconsin. In his field notes, Lyons describes how he marked his progress looking out over the very section of land that now hosts That Tree. In his journal, he writes, "Set a bur oak post and raised a mound of earth for corner to section. Sand, rolling, 1st rate prairie, dry and arable."

I can almost see him pausing to admire a lone oak standing proudly on a knoll. It's possible he even gazed upon the very tree that deposited the acorn which fathered That Tree. Somehow, That Tree stands today as a remnant and reminder of our historical past, a sentinel of the prairie.

I learned the true age of That Tree through the assistance of a local geologist who studies oak trees. He took a core sample in December of 2012 and determined that it is approximately 163 years old. He also discovered that it is hollow, but he indicated it is still very healthy and likely to thrive for years to come.

"That Tree has been here for 200 years, I'm not the guy that's going to push it over."

The chronological ownership of the land hosting That Tree goes back to 1839 when John Hawkins Rountree, an eminent and venerable pioneer settler of Grant County, first purchased the land. The land deed was passed to several owners until 1869 when John Vine took ownership. Descendants of Mr. Vine farmed the land until 1989. That's when Bob Digman purchased the property. Until Digman bought the land, the entire acreage had been in pasture. Digman's plan was to break sod and plant a crop of corn and soybeans. I asked Bob how it was that the tree was spared and he answered, "There weren't that many trees on the land and I just liked that tree." I love his coincidental reference to That Tree.

Clare Land Company LLC took ownership of the property in 1997. Family member Tim Clare who currently farms the land is a close boyhood friend. We used to hunt, fish, mountain bike, and raise all manner of young man hell together. In April of 2012, about a month into my project, Tim recounted a story to me from just before I began my photo project. Tim had hired an excavation company to remove some old fence lines and repair the waterways for seeding. On the day he came out to inspect the excavation project, the bulldozer operator asked Tim if he should push over the tree while he was at it. Clare replied, "That tree has been here for 200 years, I'm not the guy that's going to push it over". I'm confident that under Tim's ownership, That Tree will endure well past the lifetimes of Tim or I.

These encounters which could have yielded That Tree's demise serve to underscore the fragile and precarious existence of That Tree and many others growing along the fringes of agricultural properties.

Stories like these illustrate just how important it is for those of us who love the land to protect our remaining tracts of forest, prairie, and fringe habitat. It also gives me pause to consider the coincidence of my unintended adventure and how a new technology like the iPhone has inspired me to capture and share the story of this lone sentinel oak. I hope my project will inspire others to embrace a stewardship example similar to my buddy Tim's.

November 26 - Day 248

This page : (*top to bottom, left to right*)
November 26 - Day 248 : The waxing gibbous moon hangs framed amidst the gnarly branches of That Tree.
November 27 - Day 249 : Highlighted by the warm glow of sunrise, hoarfrost clings to a barbed wire fence leading up to That Tree.
November 28 - Day 250 : Stark and solemn, winter's ruinous beauty.

Facing Page :
November 29 - Day 251 : With the first glow of sunrise, cornstalks emerge from the darkness as the full moon sets beyond That Tree.

November 27 - Day 249

November 28 - Day 250

November 29 - Day 251

November 30 - Day 252 : Time for school!

December 1 - Day 253

December 2 - Day 254

December 3 - Day 255

This page : (*clockwise from top left*)
December 1 - Day 253 : Faded grasses frame That Tree on the horizon.
December 2 - Day 254 : That Tree materializes veiled in misty moors.
December 3 - Day 255 : Her familiar form emerges from another misty morning.
December 4 - Day 256 : Serpentine sunrise.

Facing page :
December 5 - Day 257 : First light once again.

December 4 - Day 256

December 5 - Day 257

December 6 - Day 258

December 7 - Day 259

December 8 - Day 260

(*top to bottom, left to right*)

December 6 - Day 258 : One of those gloomy days when the visual inspiration eluded me. Fortunately the day ended with a warm glow on the horizon.

December 7 - Day 259 : Unshakable, a weathered leaf maintains it's tenacious grasp on That Tree.

December 8 - Day 260 : Cold blue shadows, the warm glow of first light and a light dusting of snowflakes accent a fallen leaf from That Tree.

December 9 - Day 261 : Leading to That Tree.

December 10 - Day 262 : Veiled in white, colors obscured like my creative vision.

December 9 - Day 261

December 10 - Day 262

December 11 - Day 263

December 12 - Day 264

December 13 - Day 265

Previous page :

December 11 - Day 263 : I spent 45 minutes running around in 10 degree temps looking for my shot while waiting for the sunrise to light That Tree. The light got nice, I shot 5 frames, and my battery died. This is getting challenging technically and creatively!

This page : (*left to right, top to bottom*)

December 12 - Day 264 : In the shadows, the cold blue light of dawn. On That Tree, the warm glow of sunrise.

December 13 - Day 265 : Sunset casts it's warm glow over trees past and present.

December 14 - Day 266 : The 100 day countdown begins! This was shot using a wide angle adapter lens that clicks onto my iPhone via the iPro lens kit. It's a bit soft around the edges but it also offers an interestingly distorted perspective with my laying on the ground view.

Facing page : (*top three photographs, left to right*)

December 15 - Day 267 : Eerily distorted by a dangling raindrop.

December 16 - Day 268 : Textures, colors, and patterns of the season.

December 17 - Day 269 : A fold in the clouds reveals a slice of light and color over That Tree at the conclusion of a gray, gloomy day.

December 14 - Day 266

December 15 - Day 267

December 16 - Day 268

December 17 - Day 269

December 18 - Day 270

December 19 - Day 271

(*bottom two, left to right*)
December 18 - Day 270 : In a poetic scene reflecting the natural order of things, a fallen leaf from That Tree is laid to rest with an honor guard of bowing foxtail and a dusting of ice crystals.
December 19 - Day 271 : A hazy calm before the storm.

December 20 - Day 272 : Near white out conditions. Driving my truck to get to That Tree was a crazy adventure in itself. Snowmageddon, whatever! Other than the challenge of keeping my phone dry from the wet blowing snow, it was hardly the worst conditions I've been in.

December 21 - Day 273

December 22 - Day 274

December 23 - Day 275

December 24 - Day 276

(*left to right, top to bottom*)

December 21 - Day 273 : That Tree stands amidst a sculpted and wind swept landscape following yesterday's midwest blizzard. The storm deposited 14 inches of snow across the area.

December 22 - Day 274 : Footprints left in the snow by geologist Evan Larson, (left) and magazine editor Rollie Henkes (www.mrswoodsmagazine.com) lead to That Tree. They joined me very early this morning to take a core sample and gather other information about That Tree and my project for an upcoming article in Woodlands & Prairies Magazine.

December 23 - Day 275 : Harvest holdouts weather the elements from the other side of the draw.

December 24 - Day 276 : A stark and grey day.

December 25 - Day 277

December 26 - Day 278

December 27 - Day 279

December 28 - Day 280

(left to right, top to bottom)

December 25 - Day 277 : It was 1 degree above zero when I shot this at 6:15 a.m.

December 26 - Day 278 : Last night's gorgeous light has yielded to another gray day so I've opted to share the colorful photo from my sunset stroll.

December 27 - Day 279 : Sadly, the sunrise bashfully declined my invitation to join me for this morning's very early aerial photo shoot. The resulting light challenged the iPhone's ability to shoot with fast enough shutter speeds to avoid blurry images.

December 28 - Day 280 : How fragile exists a snowflake? Even more so resting like down in the delicately fringed basket of a bur oak acorn shell.

December 29 - Day 281 : A tiny snowflake amidst the coral like growth of lichen on the bark of That Tree. Shot with my inexpensive little macro eye adapter.

December 29 - Day 281

(*counter clockwise from top right*)

December 30 - Day 282 : Keeping it simple with warm early morning light and hoar-frost. My truck thermometer read -6 when I hiked out to wait for the sunlight. It was a crisply pleasant morning to watch the moonset and the sunrise.

December 31 - Day 283 : The organic flowing form of That Tree stands out against a stark and barren landscape.

January 1 - Day 284 : Sunset shadows of That Tree.

January 2 - Day 285 : Illuminated by the warm glow of sunrise, the moon sets beyond That Tree.

December 30 - Day 282

December 31 - Day 283

January 1 - Day 284

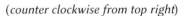

January 2 - Day 285

January 3 - Day 286

(left to right, top to bottom)

January 3 - Day 286 : Indigo shadows, deep blue skies and the colorful pastel sweep of a fading sunset.

January 4 - Day 287 : Cast against a cold blue sky, the warm light of sunrise reflects off of the weathered branches of that tree.

January 5 - Day 288 : Lovely morning. 12 degrees and sunny.

January 6 - Day 289 : Textures, lines, and hues of the predawn light.

January 4 - Day 287

January 5 - Day 288

January 6 - Day 289

This page : (*counter clockwise from top right*)
January 7 - Day 290 : Hello sun.

January 8 - Day 291 : Silhouetted against the sunrise, a leaf from That Tree hangs suspended in the tangled grasp of a gooseberry bush.

January 9 - Day 292 : An early morning shot with the old farmstead in the left background. Did some research at the register of deeds yesterday and discovered the first owner of this property was John Hawkins Rountree in 1839. The first family to build a farmstead living on the land was John Vine in 1869. His heirs continued to own the land until 1989. The house is gone but the farm buildings remain.

January 10 - Day 293 : Like microscopic ice cubes, frost crystals cling to the radicle of an acorn lying on the ground beneath That Tree.

Facing page :

January 11 - Day 294 : Normally hidden by the shady green canopy, the bare branches and today's thick misty light added drama to the scene by showcasing all of the moss and lichen thriving on the bark of That Tree. That Tree truly serves as an oasis nurturing an incredible array of living things.

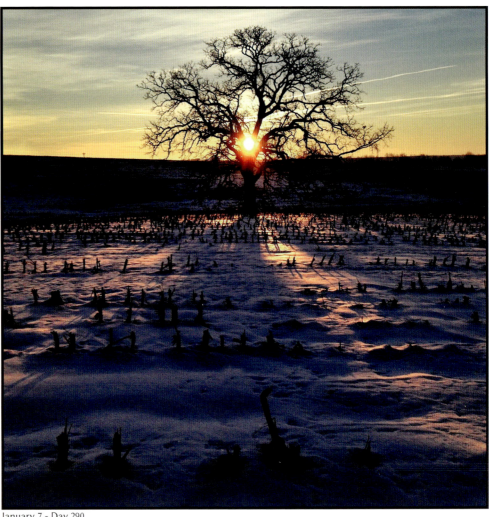

January 7 - Day 290

January 8 - Day 291

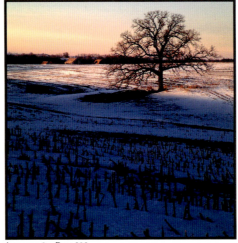

January 9 - Day 292

January 10 - Day 293

January 11 - Day 294

January 12 - Day 295

January 13 - Day 296

January 14 - Day 297

January 15 - Day 298

January 16 - Day 299

January 17 - Day 300

(*left to right, top to bottom*)

January 12 - Day 295 : The warm weather stole away all the snow and I waited all day hoping for a change in the gloomy grey light but it wasn't meant to be.

January 13 - Day 296 : I had interesting light and sky to work with this morning.

January 14 - Day 297 : Amidst the stark shadows of sunrise, a leaf from That Tree rests on a sculpted bed of crystallized snow.

January 15 - Day 298 : Frost crystals coat the grasses lining the waterway beneath That Tree.

January 16 - Day 299 : It always moves me to witness dawn's crimson light as it paints it's way down the length of That Tree at sunrise.

January 17 - Day 300 : Today is kind of a monumental milestone! Cross lighted by the sunrise, textured like course sand, and sculpted by the wind, an undulating frozen landscape leads to That Tree.

January 18 - Day 301 : An abandoned fence line points the way to That Tree's enduring presence.

January 18 - Day 301

January 19 - Day 302

January 20 - Day 303

January 21 - Day 304

Previous page :

January 19 - Day 302 : Saw this driving home from Madison last night and barely got there in time to photograph it.

This page : (*clockwise from top left*)

January 20 - Day 303 : The warm glow of sunrise defies the reality of this morning's bitter cold temperatures. Air temp, -2 degrees.

January 21 - Day 304 : Air temp, -6 degrees! Wind chill, -15! Brrrrr! My iPhone shut down after 10 frames.

And a footnote to my cold phone story, I got to That Tree before sunrise to case out a shot that I planned to capture from the south looking north. This image is looking south. When the light was just about where I wanted it, I reached in for my phone and discovered it wasn't in my pocket. Ugghhhhh! I ran the 400 frigid yards back to my truck and discovered it was sitting on my seat. By the time I got back to the tree, this is the light I had to work with. I made a couple frames of this composition and moved to my previously planned position. I shot a few frames from that spot but the light wasn't right. I moved to try a couple more options when the phone shut down on me. Seemed a good sign to call it a wrap.

January 22 - Day 305 : Dwarfed on the horizon by an expanse of cold blue sky, That Tree solemnly endures -9 degree temperatures.

January 22 - Day 305

January 23 - Day 306

January 24 - Day 307

January 25 - Day 308

This page : (*left to right, top to bottom*)
January 23 - Day 306 : A blanket of fresh falling snow cleanses the landscape obscuring That Tree in a spectral haze.
January 24 - Day 307 : Fall's remnants revealed by a January thaw.
January 25 - Day 308 : After a whirlwind trip to Chicago to work on my book project, I made it home just in time to shoot a photograph of That Tree lit by the warm glow of sunset.
January 26 - Day 309 : A familiar composition varied only by dawn's early light.

Next pages : (*left to right*)
January 27 - Day 310 : The ice storm kept me from photographing That Tree until it was almost too late. Then the visual struggle left me worried I would not capture a representative photo. When I rolled down one of my truck windows, the sheet of ice completely covered the window opening acting as a watery filter to shoot through.
January 28 - Day 311 : Warm temperatures melted yesterday's ice forming a temporary stream in the valley below That Tree.

January 26 - Day 309

January 27 - Day 310

January 28 - Day 311

January 29 - Day 312

January 30 - Day 313

This page : (*clockwise from top left*)
January 29 - Day 312 : As grand as it really is, That Tree seems so finite amidst today's misty haze.
January 30 - Day 313 : Another snowstorm blew in to dress up the landscape.
January 31 - Day 314 : Ungodly cold 4 degree air temperatures magnified by the -15 degrees wind chill challenged my iPhone's willingness to function. I settled for this shot after desperately reviving it by warming it up between two chemical hand warmers.

Facing Page :
February 1 - Day 315 : A contrasty sunset ends another bitter cold day in Wisconsin.

January 31 - Day 314

February 1 - Day 315

February 2 - Day 316

February 3 - Day 317

February 4 - Day 318

This page : (*clockwise from top left*)
February 2 - Day 316 : Sentinel Oak on a vanished prairie.

February 3 - Day 317 : Sunshine and blue skies disguise the bitter cold temperatures.

February 4 - Day 318 : I was soaking wet and frozen after laying in the snow for 30 minutes waiting for the light to get just right but my efforts were rewarded when the gloomy day ended with blue skies and a warm sunset.

February 5 - Day 319 : The color of the day was a gloomy gray! I hiked the entire circumference of That Tree from about a half mile away hoping to see an inspiring composition but in the end I settled on this stark and lonely perspective.

Facing page :

February 6 - Day 320 : Like a scene from the land of fairy, That Tree rises ethereal from the enchanted mists.

February 5 - Day 319

February 6 - Day 320

February 7 - Day 321

February 8 - Day 322

This page : (*left to right*)
February 7 - Day 321 : Framed by dried seed pods of velvetleaf plants, That Tree is hidden on the horizon by the haze of sleet and snow.
February 8 - Day 322 : I went out before sunrise and made some images I liked but they were just too gloomy for me. At around 11:30 the sun finally broke through the clouds so I decided to try and make a photo at the unlikely time of high noon.

Facing page :
February 9 - Day 323 : The cool blue break of day.

February 9 - Day 323 ⟶

February 10 - Day 324

February 11 - Day 325

February 12 - Day 326

This page : (*clockwise from top left*)

February 10 - Day 324 : A lovely fog blew in greatly improving my opportunity for an image from today's duel expeditions to photograph That Tree.

February 11 - Day 325 : It's a pleasant feeling when everything comes together. It was another gray and blustery day. I made my second visit of the day to That Tree but with the overcast pall, I was ready to resign myself to an oh-well photo. I was half way back to my truck when I took one last look at That Tree to discover a momentary break in the clouds. I ran a personal best 200m to capture this fleeting glimpse of sunlight.

February 12 - Day 326 : A brief glimmer of sunlight before winter's gloom settled in.

February 13 - Day 327 : Glowing with a frosty edged halo, a fallen leaf from That Tree is backlit by the sunrise.

Facing page :

February 14 - Day 328 : An interesting bank of cumulus clouds blew in to enhance the midday skies over That Tree.

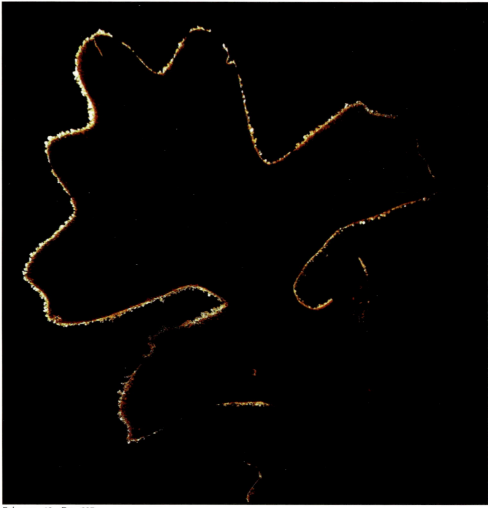

February 13 - Day 327

February 14 - Day 328

February 15 - Day 329 : That Tree and the morning sky are reflected in an icy waterway at sunrise.

February 16 - Day 330

This page : (*clockwise from top left*)

February 16 - Day 330 : Blue skies and a lovely sunrise are usually quite inspiring. The visual conundrum of this project though is such that everyday is feeling like that of Bill Murray's charcter in Groundhog Day. Then I discovered my daily epiphany as That Tree was photo bombed by a distant companion. Perfect!

February 17 - Day 331 : Shadows, silhouettes and sun bursts.

February 18 - Day 332 : Gnarled by seasons and warmed by a fading glow, That Tree stands against a timeless winter sky.

February 19 - Day 333 : It was a howling, blowing snow morning. Air temp, 1 degree. Wind chill -19. Experiential rating, perfect!

Facing page :

February 20 - Day 334 : Contrasty, cold and colorful! It was a brisk but sunny -2 when my publishing partner Warren Winter and I headed out to wait for this morning's sunrise. I photographed That Tree and he photographed me. (See the inside front and inside rear flaps)

February 17 - Day 331

February 19 - Day 333

February 18 - Day 332

February 20 - Day 334

February 21 - Day 335 : Destined to be the heart of a future oak, an acorn and a fallen leaf are exposed by the recent thaw. By the end of the day, they are forecast to be buried under a fresh blanket of 6 to 8 inches of snow.

This page : (*clockwise from top left*)
February 22 - Day 336 : Rooted in a land once dominated by tall grass prairie and oak savanna, That Tree stands as a reminder of what once was.
February 23 - Day 337 : I found myself cradled in her enduring embrace for a delightfully lofty perspective.
February 24 - Day 338 : Bold blue skies highlight hoarfrost crystals coating the outer branches of That Tree.
February 25 - Day 339 : The setting sun casts warm light over a stark landscape.

Facing page :
February 26 - Day 340 : Witnessing the pastel hues, wispy tendrils, and heart warming glow of last night's sunset, my gloomy morning photos just didn't inspire me.

February 22 - Day 336

February 23 - Day 337

February 25 - Day 339

February 24 - Day 338

February 26 - Day 340

February 27 - Day 341 : An ink drawing landscape sketched on a fresh blanket of snow.

February 28 - Day 342

March 1 - Day 343

This page : (*left to right*)
February 28 - Day 342 : With the grayness of the day making me blue, I opted to embrace the cool hues of dusk to dress up a familiar scene.
March 1 - Day 343 : I had a crazy busy day which concluded with a fun interview with the Sierra Club. I made a late trek out to shoot my tree photo and discovered this record of last night's acorn foraging feast by the deer.

Facing page :
March 2 - Day 344 : Just before sunrise, a waning moon hangs in the morning sky framed by the gnarly branches of That Tree.

March 2 - Day 344 ⟶

March 3 - Day 345

March 4 - Day 346

This page : (*counter clockwise from top right*)
March 3 - Day 345 : Looking so hard for that perfect image has made me blind to the simple beauty of first light, a pastoral landscape and the enduring presence of a sentinel oak.
March 4 - Day 346 : My occasional fortune with lighting makes me wonder about the power of That Tree. I spent an hour wandering visually, settling down to wait and watch. The sky opened up with color and light allowing me to capture this scene. The sky closed and I walked back to reality.
March 5 - Day 347 : Winter's lingering grasp leaves That Tree standing tall on a landscape whitewashed with new fallen snow.

Facing page :
March 6 - Day 348 : I had an incredible day. Seems fitting that it concluded with this glorious sunset over That Tree.

March 5 - Day 347

March 6 - Day 348 ⟶

March 7 - Day 349 : The silent presence of a deer's journey, like mine, drawn to That Tree.

March 8 - Day 350

March 9 - Day 351

March 10 - Day 352

This page : (*clockwise from top left*)

March 8 - Day 350 : With frost crystals twinkling on the wilted grasses, That Tree is dwarfed on the horizon against a sunny blue sky.

March 9 - Day 351 : It was early evening before I headed out in the cold rainy weather seeking today's photo. Extremely difficult shooting conditions.

March 10 - Day 352 : Like the seasonal passing of time, a transient river carries away winter's veil.

March 11 - Day 353 : A gray day ends with my late afternoon visit to That Tree in search of another photo. My quest fulfilled by a simple discovery.

March 12 - Day 354

March 11 - Day 353

March 12 - Day 354 : Dawn broke gray and somber on a landscape dusted with a fresh snowfall. The only constant, That Tree's enduring presence.

Facing page :
March 13 - Day 355 : After days of gloom, it's refreshing to share a cold but colorful perspective.

Next pages : (*left to right*)
March 14 - Day 356 : That Tree stands finite against the elements, shrouded in the grips of a late season snowstorm.
March 15 - Day 357 : Remnants revealed, like winter, soon departed.

March 13 - Day 355

March 14 - Day 356

March 15 - Day 357

March 16 - Day 358

March 17 - Day 359

This page : (*clockwise from top left*)
March 16 - Day 358 : It was another gray day until Amber Arnold of the Wisconsin State Journal showed up to inspire a brief break in the clouds giving us both some nice light to work with.
March 17 - Day 359 : Textured beams, crimson light, and deep blue skies. Lovely morning.
March 18 - Day 360 : Spent an interesting day shooting a segment on my tree project with a producer from Iowa Public Television. The winter weather yielded nice photo opportunities for both of us.

Facing page :
March 19 - Day 361 : Dawn broke on a frigid single digit morning with two sundogs dancing on the horizon with That Tree.

March 18 - Day 360

March 19 - Day 361 ⟶

March 20 - Day 362   March 21 - Day 363

This page : (*left to right*)
March 20 - Day 362 : Warm first rays of sunlight cast a magenta glow onto snowdrifts lining the valley below That Tree. Hard to believe it's the first day of spring.
March 21 - Day 363 : I sat there this morning watching the sun paint its crimson glow down the length of That Tree. Then it reached out to light these withered corn volunteers too.

Facing page :
March 22 - Day 364 : I walked to That Tree pondering my shot. I made several images toying with a landscape sculpted by wind and weather. Then I realized that the light was going to be gorgeous and conducive to closing the circle with a composition I captured for my first photo on January 20, 2012. I only had to wait for the sun's magic.

March 22 - Day 364

March 23 - Day 365

The reward of the day and conclusion of what has been an incredibly rewarding project. That Tree and I cannot thank you enough for making this such an amazing experience! I am truly thankful to all.

(In alphabetical order) Gerard Abing, Willie Allen, Josette Andre, Lance Andre, Traci Andre, Wilbur B. Austin, Michele Bartels, Rob Bell, Natalee Berg, Richard Biechler, Linda Billings, Jane Boutelle, John Boutelle, John A. Brennan, Regina Brennan, Jessica Brogley, Jane Munden Brown, Joe Brown, Bibi Burke, Kevin Butson, Mary Butson, Shannon Butson, Bruce Canny, Anthony F. Carbone, Jaydon A. Carbone, Dave Carnahan, Ellen Carnahan, Nick Carnahan, Jim Cerro, Brent Christianson, Rebecca Christianson, Justin Clare, Matthew Clare, Ryan Clare, Tim Clare, Gary A. Clark, Paula Connors, Pete Corby, Ben Cramer, Joan Cramer, Matt Cramer, Barbara W. Cullen, Brenden Cullen, Cody Cushman, Darwin Cushman, James Cushman, Karla Egan-Dailey, Dennis Deery, Dona Deery, John B. Donovan, Noelle Dowling, Kyle Ebbe, Kim Egan, Kim Wisdom-Egan, Cathy Elwell, Victor Emanuel, Fred Failmezger, Stephanie Failmezger, Nancy Felker, Alan Lee (Albone) Flesch, Bill Flesch, Andrew Frigo, Ann Frigo, Thomas J. Goodman, Jessie L. Goodwin, Melissa Grohs, Bill Grutz, Neal Gunter, David S. Hartig, Evan Hartig,

Joyce Hartig, Jill Hasker, Brady Headington, Cheryl Hefty, Mike Hefty, Nick Hefty, Dennis Helbing, Kathryn A. Hess, Anita Highland, Keli Highland, Mark Highland, Linda Hildreth, Andy Hirsch, Alex Hirsch, Brittany Hirsch, Cassandra Hirsch, Dave Hirsch, Denee Hirsch, Emily Hirsch, Kay Hirsch, John Hirsch, Jon Hirsch, Teresa Hirsch, Tristan Hirsch, Vicki Hirsch, Paul L. Hoffman, Jane Howe, Patti Joyce, Sandra Kaisely, Kathy Kessler, Curt Kiessling, Sandy Kilburg, Jason Klein, Carol Kliebenstenstein, Don Kinsley, Rita Kinsley, Bill Koepcke, Lora Kohnlein, Joe Kopp, Kathy Kopp, Wes Kopp, James Kraus, Sue E. Kraus, Jon Kreiss, Molly Kreiss, Lisa Kress, Christopher Paul Kruger, Ben Kuhls, Eric Kuhls, Lisa M. Kuhls, Braelyn Kuro, James Kuro, Trista Kuro, John W. LaCoste, Velda J. LaCoste, Brady Lawinger, Brooke Lawinger, Megan Lawinger, Adrian Lee, DeAnne Leffler, Glen Leffler, Ross Lemery, Shane P. Lenane, Ali Levasseur, Sam LoBianco, Gabe Loeffelholz, Joyce Loeffelholz, Jennie Loney, Emily Lubcke, Jaxin Mackienruf, Kelly McBride, Kerry McCabe, Mary Kay McCarthy, Leslie McDermott, Dean Marcinkowski, Lola Marcinkowski, Jacqui Finken Meach, Jeff Mergen, Julie Tyess-Michek, Esther Mihm, Richard J. Mihm, Brian Molle, Deb Molle, Mary Moody, Connie M. Moran, Laura Morland, Tracy Morland, Retha Mulrooney, Kathy Murphy, Tim Murphy, Denise Nelson, Kathy Neumeister, Lexi Neumeister, Chris Neuzil, Pam Nodolf, Tom Nodolf, Joseph Nolan, James Nordorft, Phyllis Nordorft, Barry Nudd, Linda Nudd, Jan Ochoa, Jess Ochoa, Mateo Ochoa, Lori Oglesby, Paul Opperman, Cherylin Parrilli, David Parrilli, Julie Parrilli, Finn Patenaude, Harper Patenaude, Joel Patenaude, Diane Paynter, Greg Pekas, Blake Peterson, Nolan Peterson, Randy Peterson, Adam Pick, Jared Pick, Peter Pitsker, Jeremy Portje, Anne Potter, Ralph Potter, Kassandra Powell, Brian Powers, Jill Powers, Kyle Powers, Ruth Powers, Arnie Rawson, Alyson Reeves, Adam Reinstein, Fern Reinstein, Jes Reyerson, Nathan Richardson, Cory Ritterbusch, Paula Romeo, Jackie Ruf, Margaret Ruf, Bob Runde, Jean Runde, M. Schief, Steven Schleuning, David Schmit, Deb Schmitt, David Schoonover, David Schramm, Jaroslav L. Sebek, Sandy Sebek, Cyrena Sexton, Miranda Sexton, Darby Shea-Kruser, April Simmons, Ryan Simmons, Norma Sliger, Amelia Spahn, Jeff Spahn, Sherry Spahn, Sullivan Spahn, Casey Spensley, Ardith Stark, Jim Stark, Pam Stark, Alexis Stecklein, Gavin Stecklein, Johanna Stecklein, Shaun Stecklein, Karl Steichen, Patricia J. Steiner, Doug Stephens, Tammy Salmon-Stephens, Joyce Stoffel, William Stoffel, Chris Sweda, Jack Taylor, Marilyn J. Taylor, Seth Taylor, Tracy Ternes, Julie Tess-Michek, Jonathan Thoreson, Jennifer Tigges, Ronald Tigges, Willie Tigges, Kathy Topel, Larry Trine, Beth Triplett, Gene Tully, Jane Tully, Mary Beth Tully, Ashley Tyson, Colton Tyson, Courtney Tyson, Jason Tyson, Kara Tyson, Olivia Tyson, Markus Uitz, Dean Upton, Jean Upton, Nancy Ware, Daniel J. Weitz, Elaine Wheeler, Stephen "Sam" Wilson, Warren Winter, Corinna A. Wolfe, Gary J. Wolfe, Mary Wunderlin, Dan Wyatt, Laura Wyatt, Alyssa Zasada, Amanda Zasada, Michelle Zasada, John Zuehlke, Molly Zuehlke.

The Ornaments
And they came from miles around.

As the last couple months of my project were winding down, I kept receiving messages from fellow photographers asking me what I was planning to shoot for the final picture. I had no idea.

Soon I started receiving messages from some of my most dedicated followers who were forlorn at the approaching end of the project and disappointed that they couldn't attend the final photo shoot. Their messages expressed sincerely how much they would miss my daily pictures of That Tree. Others stated that my photos were like a daily devotional. The pictures offered them inspiration and hope and they encouraged me to continue my project indefinitely. After nearly a solid year of dedication to this project, I can assure you that wasn't going to happen! Well, maybe not. We'll see.

I was both stunned and honored by how engaged people had become with That Tree. Realizing there was an opportunity to create an epic group photo of That Tree fans, I decided to create a Facebook event inviting That Tree's many fans and followers to join me for a final group photo with That Tree.

It wasn't long after I announced the group photo gathering that I received a note from my friend and fellow artist Louise Kames telling me she would miss the photo shoot due to a scheduling conflict. She asked if she could submit an ornament or photo to hang on the tree to represent her in the photo. My thought was, "What a fantastic idea".

Her idea inspired several other followers to submit ornaments and photos as well. More than two-dozen fans took the time and care to create a variety of interesting and moving ornaments. I hung and photographed each one prior to the final group photo.

Ornaments came from as far away as Kildare, Ireland where Geraldine Gahan gathered leaves from her 200 year-old oak to include in a hand bound card along with photos of her storied tree.

One of my favorite contributions came from my friend Ryan Wetley. Ryan, a young man and veteran I respect greatly, included this message with his ornament for That Tree's photo. "This Boston Red Sox cap is one of my most prized possessions... also one of my most recognizable ones... It's been to 6 continents with me to include in combat in Baghdad. I would be honored to have it as part of the tree photo!" I was humbled that he entrusted his cap to me for inclusion in the final group photo.

I was hoping for a big turn out but realistically speaking, how many people would actually drive way out to the middle of southwest Wisconsin to pose with a tree in a muddy cornfield? Quite a few it turned out.

And they came from miles around, some from hundreds of miles, in fact, including participants from Milwaukee, Chicago and Minneapolis. At 4:00 p.m. on March 23, 2013, almost 300 people, a dozen dogs, and a handful of journalists trudged through ankle deep mud and melting snow to pose with That Tree.

My friend Ross Lemery summed up the gathering describing the event as, "the greatest outpouring of support he had ever seen for someone who wasn't dead or dying."

Diane Weis of Omaha, Nebraska

In memory of Sheila Hargrave of Bellevue, Iowa

Lisa "Hoot" Evers of Charlotte, North Carolina

Renate Langan of Cedar Rapids, Iowa

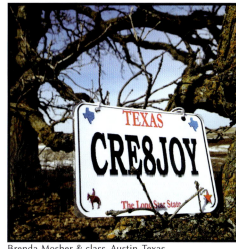

Brenda Mosher & class, Austin, Texas

Beverly Foote of Charleston, Illinois

Kirstin Pope of Dubuque, Iowa in honor of Mike Metz

Christina Curras of Platteville, Wisconsin

Sue Kroll-Barry of Anchorage, Alaska

Bob & Donna Dwyer of Pharr, Texas

St. Joseph Catholic High School students of Bryan, TX.

Louise Kames of Dubuque, Iowa

Amy Ruf & Greg Vann of Boulder, Colorado

Sydney Ruf-Wong & Simone Pilgaard-Hansen, Denmark

Keith & Marie Dotseth of St. Paul, Minnesota

Steve & Tiffany Warmowski of Jacksonville, Illinois

Riley Gilmore III of Orangeville, California

Patty Campbell Blaszak of Bryan, Texas

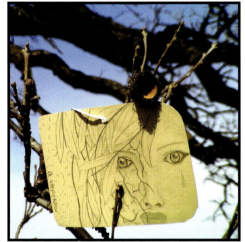

Kris & Lauren Orr of Princeton, New Jersey

Renate Langan of Cedar Rapids, Iowa

Bridget Maruska & family of Sturgeon Lake, MN.

Heidi Stoffel Kroner & family of Johnston, Iowa

Ryan Wetley of Sparta, Wisconsin

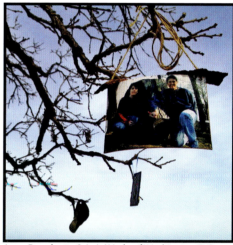

Anne Dougherty & Lois Wesly of Washington D.C.

Geraldine Gahan of Kildare, Ireland

Anna Reuter of Platteville, Wisconsin

Judy Kesser of Franklin, Wisconsin

Closing Thoughts
Vision, Transformation & Healing

As the project drew to a close, I found myself sitting there with my back against my old friend hoping she might share her transcendent wisdom. I realized the images within these pages represent more than just the photos I made every day of a tree. They represent commitment, sacrifice, personal growth, and healing. They represent my own personal and professional transformation.

Life has a way of shaking things up when you get too comfortable. First in 2006, I felt like I'd been hit by a truck after I unexpectedly lost my job. Then, in October 2011, my life was turned upside down when I was literally hit by a truck. I was nearly killed when the chutes from the back of a concrete mixer truck crashed through my windshield. The chutes ripped the roof off my truck, broke the headrest off of my seat, and knocked me unconscious. The EMT's who responded couldn't believe I was alive. For months following the crash, I was unable to work. I had memory issues. I lost my drive and ambition.

When I committed to make a daily photo of That Tree starting on March 24th, I had no idea I would be committing myself to do so for an entire year. I had no idea what a professionally transformative and personally therapeutic experience my daily commitment to That Tree would be. It just happened. I really didn't ponder the lifestyle sacrifices it would require, and I definitely didn't consider the sacrifices my family would have to make in order for me to succeed. There would be no family vacation. No western ski trip with my buddies. The list goes on and on. I owe my family a big thank you for their understanding.

The peaceful contemplative opportunities provided by my daily photo visits actually motivated me to sometimes visit That Tree with no goal of making pictures at all. These were just opportunities to relax and clear my mind.

The sacrifices were great but the rewards were tremendous too. My evolution as a photographer was transformative. That Tree inspired me to have a greater appreciation for the simple things. She also taught me to slow down and take on a more considered approach to photography. I learned to become more sensitive to the subtle changes in light, the details and the textures. When I discovered a scene, situation, or moment that made me confident that I had made a worthy picture for the day, it was incredibly rewarding. That Tree helped me to heal. Something I needed more than I think I realized at the time.

Nearing the conclusion of my project, I was sitting by That Tree experiencing a tremendous range of emotions, everything from satisfaction to sadness. I could never have intentionally conceived of a project that would yield as many challenges and rewards as That Tree has. Nor could I have envisioned the worldwide interest this project would generate. It amazes me how a simple photo of a lone oak tree taken with an iPhone could inspire such a dramatic outcome.

I want my viewers to put themselves in my place on the landscape mesmerized by the sunset while listening to the blackbird's song. I want them to hear and feel the wind whispering through the branches. I hope people will take time to look for the deeper moments in life, the things that really shape and give meaning to their lives and appreciate the almost, but not quite, hidden beauty that abounds endlessly all around us.